CATS
HAVE NO MASTERS ... JUST FRIENDS

CATS
HAVE NO MASTERS ... JUST FRIENDS

An Investigation into the Feline Mind
by KAREN ANDERSON

WILLOW CREEK PRESS

Minocqua, Wisconsin

© 1998, text by Karen Anderson

Published by WILLOW CREEK PRESS
P.O. Box 147
Minocqua, Wisconsin 54548

Designed by Heather M. McElwain

PHOTOGRAPHY CREDITS:
Norvia Behling: 10, 21, 24 right, 26 (both), 27, 34 right, 37 left, 38 right, 39 left, 40 left, 41 left, 41 middle, 47, 51 right, 54, 57, 61 right, 63 left, 64 left, 66, 67, 69 left, 74 left, 78 left, 80 left, 82 (both), 83, 84 (both), 88 right, 95, 97 right, 99, 100, 106, 109; Chris Boylan/ Unicorn Stock: 53; Alan & Sandy Carey: 4, 9, 29, 42, 44, 45, 55, 59, 62 left, 71, 77, 89 left, 91 left; Walter Chandoha: 86, 110; Doug Dasher/Uniphoto: 15; Joel Dexter/Unicorn Stock: 70; Doemmrich/Uniphoto: 96; David M. Doody/Uniphoto: 74 right, 75; Diane Ensign/Green Agency: 6-7, 8, 31, 80 right, 104; William B. Folsom: 32 left, 39 right, 91 right; W.R. Green/Green Agency: 85; Ed Harp/Unicorn Stock: 20; James A. Hays/Unicorn Stock: 97 left; V. E. Horne/Unicorn Stock: 76; Martin R. Jones/Unicorn Stock: 32 right; Ron Kimball/Hillstrom Stock: 17; Erika Klass/Hillstrom Stock: 37 right; Chris Luneski/ Image Cascade: 11, 16, 56, 98; Steve and Dave Maslowski/Maslowski Photo: 78 right; Bonnie Nance/Nance Photography: 18, 25, 34 left, 35 left, 38 left, 46, 50, 61 left, 62 right, 63 right, 68, 69 right, 87, 89 right, 94, 101, 102, 103, 105, 107, 108; Louisa Preston/ Hillstrom/AppaLight Stock: 12, 35 right, 51 left, 73; Hazel Schmeiser/ Unicorn Stock: 41 right, 90 (both); Larry Stanley/Unicorn Stock: 24 left; Terry Wild Studio/ Uniphoto: 14, 33, 60; D. Bunde/Unicorn Stock: 58; Terry Way/Uniphoto: 36; Sally Weigand/Hillstrom Stock: 13, 40 right, 81, 88 left, 92, 93; Jean Wentworth: 2, 5, 28 (both), 30, 48 (both), 49, 52, 64 right, 65, 72, 79; Gale Zucker 22-23.

For information on other Willow Creek titles, call 1-800-850-9453

Library of Congress Cataloging-in-Publication Data
Anderson, Karen, 1958-
    Cats have no masters--just friends : an investigation into the feline mind / by Karen Anderson.
        p.   cm.
    ISBN 1-57223-135-1
    1. Cats--Behavior. 2. Cats--Psychology. I. Title.
    SF446.5.A528 1998
636.8'088'7--dc21   98-2793
                                                      CIP

Printed in Canada

I dedicate this book to my husband, Craig . . .
and to Buttons, our beloved feline

ACKNOWLEDGMENTS

Thanks to everyone at Willow Creek Press, especially Tom Petrie for catching my vision and running with it; Laura Evert for her managerial editing and careful, helpful, enthusiastic handling of the manuscript; and Heather McElwain for her great design sense, all of which have contributed to a book I am very proud of. Thanks also to the many photographers who supplied awesome and amazing cat photos for the book, bringing rich illustration to the text.

I wish to thank Ed Marquand for the generous spirit in which he and Manine Golden read my unfinished manuscript, strongly encouraged its completion and offered excellent advice on seeking publication. (I fondly recall the day about three years ago, when a certain electrician worked in your office and told you of a cat book in the making.)

A huge thank-you to Elissa Kamins for coming alongside to create charming sketches and watercolors of cats in and around my world, which spurred me on.

Several cat-loving individuals come to mind when I think of the people whose relationships with cats I admire. These folks have inspired me—and surely others—by their wise, sensitive and loving ways with cats. Much applause for Karen Scott, Jason Scott, Maxine Nicklos, Katrina Haines, Annie Burnham and Dawn Hammontre. I must honor as well the late James Herriot, animal lover extraordinaire and devoted veterinarian whose beautiful book, *Cat Stories*, serves continually to remind me how incredible cats truly are and how many people still need to know!

In thankful praise of all felines everywhere, I pay particular tribute to the memorable cats I have had the privilege of meeting over the years—for a short while or luxuriously longer—especially Sabrina, Java, Mozart, Tarzan, Pansy, Wampus, Esther, Caleb, Daisy, Butterscotch, Mosha, Pickity, Bentley, Ocean, Tootsie, Lipton, Maggie, Checkers, Beulah, Jingles, Kiki, Rosalie, Alice, Noel and Buttons.

Special thanks to Wes and Eunice Christensen, Dianne Bratz, Susan Staple and Margaret, Myrt, Jan and John, Janine and Bob, Annie, Becky, Toni, Dawn, Terri, Max, Charnell and Patty for their cheerleading and solid affirmations along the way.

And last on the list but first in my heart, I thank deeply and lovingly my husband, Craig Anderson—a true feline advocate—for believing in me and this project throughout every step and for demonstrating it faithfully. (I love you more than ever . . .)

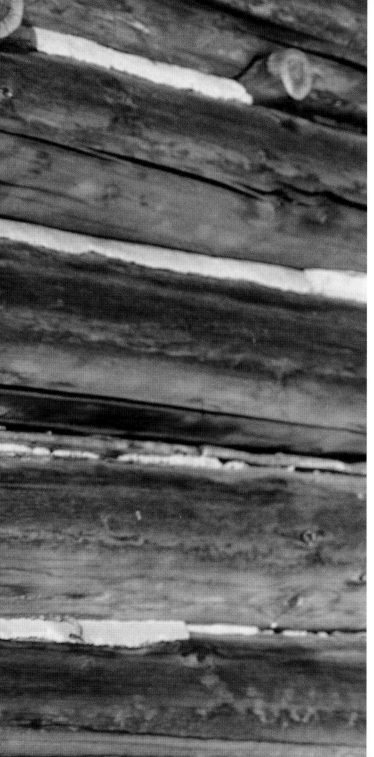

TABLE OF CONTENTS

INTRODUCTION

Don't Treat Your Cat Like a Dog

DO YOU SOMETIMES WISH that cats were more like dogs? Have you tried in vain to train your cat? Are you wondering if there's something wrong with him? Do you seriously question whether or not the cat in your life even *likes* you? Perhaps you keep hoping your kitty will learn a lesson or two from a nearby dog and behave a little more responsively. Maybe you and your cat are in a rut and you need fresh insight. Or, it could be that you already enjoy a satisfying relationship with your cat and you simply want to make it better. If you are nodding "yes" to any of this, the book you're holding is just for you.

Some people look down upon cats because they are so catlike and so very *un*doglike. A cat can sense this . . . and here is where the trouble usually starts. The subtle, melancholy cat is often treated with slight disrespect, while the outgoing, obedient dog is praised as "man's best friend." Cats can hardly blossom under this unfortunate burden! The Feline has been handed a pretty bad rap over the years; sometimes cats deserve it, but many times not. Cartoon cats (sorry, Garfield) haven't helped the situation. Too often, only the very worst parts of the feline personality are portrayed . . . rarely showing us how wonderful the cat can be. Cats remain loved by oodles of devoted "cat people," misunderstood and under-appreciated by countless others.

A Little Misunderstanding

CATS ARE ACCUSED OF being lazy, aloof and untrainable. These are only myths — but plenty of people believe them! This erroneous thinking results in one of two things: either kitty is written-off as simply being the way cats are, and never trained and nurtured properly; or kitty endures much scolding and rebuking for not measuring up. With either course, the cat is terribly unhappy and the cat owner decidedly dissatisfied — unaware that life with kitty can be any other way. There *is* another way!

Trying to train or educate your cat inappropriately will accomplish nothing more than taking the cat's spirit and spunk away, and that's what you want to avoid. In fact, while trying to reform the cat, you may have used a few doggie methods on a furry, four-legged feline, hoping to whip him or her into shape! (Tisk, tisk.) Perhaps you relate more to dogs and this has come natural to you.

If you're waiting for your cat to become more like a dog, you'll be waiting a long, long time (okay, forever). Kitty won't start behaving like a dog any more than a goldfish will start behaving like a hamster. And no, Kitty doesn't pick up dog traits by osmosis either. Not that he or she would *want* to. Your cat is actually very happy being a cat and wants nothing more than to show you what it means to be feline. Cats and dogs have been lumped together in people's minds for years, as if they have anything in common besides two ears, two eyes, four legs and a tail! Actually, they are drastically different.

Once a cat always a cat . . . but this certainly doesn't mean that your cat cannot become more responsive and cooperative. You don't need to settle for shredded furniture, a cat with a disgruntled personality or a kitty who never leaves the sofa. Maybe you've tried lots of techniques with your cat and you're not getting the results you'd hoped for. You run into cat-lovers everywhere, but *your* cat causes you far more grief than joy!

"You don't need to settle for shredded furniture, a cat with a disgruntled personality or a kitty who never leaves the sofa."

A Mishandled Cat

A CAT WHO IS UNAFFECTIONATE, quite mischievous or downright mean is probably suffering from mishandling by someone in their life. A cat will react to mishandling. You might win a battle or two along the way, but you'll certainly lose the war! Part Two of this book will lead you through five areas in a cat's life and the potential ways in which cats are mishandled by the humans in their lives. Grasping these simple concepts is essential to a pleasant and rewarding life with your cat. Otherwise, your kitty will most likely become unhappy or even miserable, and you will miss out on the truly awesome attributes of the feline. Amazingly, for the sake of self-preservation, a cat will try to comply with some of your tough demands . . . but overall, she or he will fade to a most unsatisfactory kitty citizen. If the cat in your life looks anything like one of the following descriptions . . . it's time to find out why and correct the problem so that you and your cat can start living together and loving it!

THE LETHARGIC CAT
This kitty is easily mistaken for being sick, depressed or just plain dull. It mostly lies around in an apathetic, uninterested state . . . having pretty much given up on any stimulating human involvement.

THE MEAN CAT
A cat who is unhappy may lash out often at his handler (and usually everyone else) with claws and teeth. This kitty could be enduring rough play, "spankings" or other kitty-raising taboos — he feels attacked by the humans in his life.

THE FRIGHTENED CAT
Some cats become literal "scardey-cats." These cats think all humans are cat murderers! They creep through their cowardly little lives believing they're barely escaping torture or death. Incidents of mishandling early in life or poor nurturing can be the cause.

THE NAUGHTY CAT
Still other cats seem to be competing for the title of most naughty cat in the world. This kitty misbehaves continually (knocking things over purposely, having an "attitude," etc.) and its owner tries to discipline him or her . . . often using the wrong methods. The cat gets mad and misbehaves all the more! An especially naughty cat can also be suffering from neglect or extreme stress among the humans in the house.

A NEW APPROACH

Do you see the cat in your life in one of those descriptions? If so, there's a good chance that your kitty is protesting about something going on around him or to him. You may be treating your cat more like a dog (or some other animal). Your methods may need some fine tuning or even a complete overhaul. You need a new approach. You need help!

This book will show you what it means to treat a cat like a cat . . . and why a cat loves it so much. You will also learn what not to do and why. If you want your cat to be a happy, pleasant, contributing little member of your household you'll want to avoid some things and over-do others. Once you get the hang of this, you'll find that sharing your home with a cat is downright fun and extremely rewarding! You will better tolerate your friends' and neighbors' cats, too.

You've heard it said that cats are mysterious creatures and cannot be figured out. That's true to a point, but there's nothing mysterious about the universal likes and dislikes of cats. Understand thy cat!

It is time to celebrate the cat. Push all dog notions (temporarily) aside. Embrace their differences! Apologize to kitty for disrespect and mishandling. Declare a truce. Find out what you've been missing by not treating your cat like a cat. You will be utterly amazed. Your cat will start responding to you. Not as a dog would, and not necessarily as the cat next door or the cat of your dreams. But before your very eyes, the cat in your life will begin to transform.

RESPECT THY CAT

IT REALLY COMES DOWN to respect. When kitty begins to feel your loving acceptance and approval, you will have quite the marvelous cat on your hands. A cat must be allowed and encouraged to be a *cat*, and everyone's going to be happier. Kitty will sense it and give it his all to win your friendship . . . and there's nothing like friendship with a cat. Most dogs worship their master because it's the right thing to do. A cat, by contrast, will *choose* to be your devoted friend.

Cats actually crave human contact. They are not nearly as independent as you might think. A cat possesses a very delicate spirit but a strong will. When treated properly, they gain confidence and trust . . .

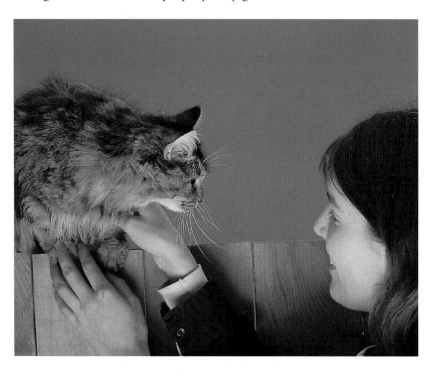

and blossom into delightful pets. Cats have a lot to offer and sincerely want to become your best friend. Don't miss the subtle signals they display. Remember to assume that your cat is longing for a mutually satisfying relationship with you . . . even though she may not show it in a way you're used to.

The feline temperament requires loving affirmation and daily interaction. Cats are smart and love to be included in human affairs . . . but a cat won't relate to *you* unless you take the lead and relate to *it* first. Cats must be assured that you really, really, really want to spend time with them. They are insecure when it comes to our affection and love.

Every cat is unique and special and quite unpredictable. The cat is at the same time complex and simple. Wild and domestic. Mysterious yet completely honest. Self-sufficient but needy. Cats are fascinating. The really great thing is that they let us into their world. If your cat doesn't already, he may soon be planting "kitty kisses" on your cheek and coming more often when you call him. He might chit-chat meaningfully with you and greet you at the door and may even follow you from room to room. You'll know that you are beginning to treat your cat like a cat when it can't wait to curl up on your lap or it asks you for one of your fabulous kitty massages.

Hopefully you are now a bit curious about how to treat your cat like it wants to be treated. The following pages will tell you how to do more than just that. Your reward will be a new relationship with your feline — a relationship that goes beyond master and pet to best friends.

PART ONE

The Cat in Your Life

P ART ONE WILL HELP to unravel a few of the more puzzling feline behavioral mysteries by way of contrasting cats with dogs. When striving to understand the feline, it is helpful to clarify what cats are not as well as to learn what cats are. Dogs and cats do share a few animal traits, of course, but for the sake of becoming an expert on cats, the next chapters will focus on the significant differences between the two, information that will prove helpful toward forging a more rewarding relationship with your feline.

This section ends with the dispelling of three popular cat myths that have been circling about for generations, and really do need to be cleared up! If you're going to try reaching out to your cat in new ways, it's critical to your success to recognize the "toxic cat beliefs" that may be lurking somewhere in the recesses of your mind . . . so that this journey into cat friendship can begin with a fresh start.

CHAPTER ONE

Dogs and Cats — A Different Kind of Love

THE MOST OBVIOUS DIFFERENCE between dogs and cats (and the biggest complaint from cat owners) is the cat's refusal to cooperate. Where is the eagerness to obey . . . the thrill of pleasing the master? The beloved dog, on the other hand, practically lives to obey. Well, there's good reason. In the wild, dogs live in tightly organized packs. They live under a strong "group ethic." Survival depends on complete cooperation with all pack members and absolute obedience to the "Top Dog."

FOLLOW THE LEADER

PET DOGS HAVE NOT shaken this ancient pack mentality. A domestic dog sees his or her owner as none other than the almost-worshipped "Top Dog." Tough shoes to fill, but dogs make it so easy for us. Wired into every canine is a phenomenal allegiance to the leader. Nothing in a dog's life is more important than pleasing its master. Dogs are driven to obey. They actually *like* it.

Can you even imagine a cat with this mission in life? Cats pride themselves on having minds of their own. (And incidentally, they love to change them.) Feline society has no formal group ethic. Cats are not antisocial, but they don't feel a need to cooperate the way dogs do. Instinct tells a cat to perform solo. A cat is a free spirit from its cool little nose to the tip of its fluffy tail.

As far as getting their basic needs met, it's pretty much every cat for himself. This all adds up to a creature who is programmed to do it's own thing. A domestic cat has zero interest in obedience for obedience sake. Following orders is meaningless to a cat. This is why your cat looks so puzzled when you order him to follow you or move or jump down or stay. You can ask a cat to do anything. If he sees something in it for him (including friendship with you), you might get the response you hoped for.

"A cat is a free spirit from its cool little nose
to the tip of its fluffy tail."

It Never Hurts to Ask

H AVE YOU NOTICED THAT cats don't give up easily? Whether it's asking to go outside at midnight when you *never* let him out, or pleading for a taste of the raw meat that you *never* let him have, your kitty is amazingly persistent when it comes to asking for things he wants. Some people assume that this means cats are not smart, when it actually may point to something altogether different. Cats are eternal optimists. Even in the face of being told a hundred times "NO," they often refuse to give up. Instead of looking upon this as a character flaw, try to view it as a positive attribute; they are forever hopeful creatures, and they figure it never hurts to ask.

CATS HAVE NO MASTERS ... ONLY FRIENDS

WHEN IS THE LAST time you called a cat and it came? Perhaps it hunkered down further or looked the other way or darted off altogether. None of these responses would be abnormal for a cat. One commands a dog. One *asks* a cat. Kitty will do what kitty wants to do. But kitty is ten times more likely to respond favorably if you treat him or her as a respected friend! A cat has no master ... only friends.

Dogs are infamous for their unconditional love. And you must admit it — that kind of love does wonders for building up a person's self-esteem. Usually, a dog considers you a friend from the outset. Even in the face of a surprising amount of mishandling or neglect, the dog's fierce loyalty endures. Dogs don't seem to have a selfish bone in their bodies. The canine persuasion knows nothing of the "I'll scratch your back if you scratch mine" mentality.

And unlike cats, dogs do not seem to be easily offended. If so, they conceal their emotions well. A dog's exuberant disposition never seems to fade. It's almost as if a dog knows that too much fussing would jeopardize "pack-solidarity."

"Kitty will do what kitty wants to do."

Feline feelings are easily bruised. Cats need to be apologized to often and offered gentle explanations for mistakes made. Some cats even charmingly respond with a "that's okay . . . I forgive you" gesture. Let kitty know you're sorry, and once again kitty's faith in you will be restored. When your cat becomes convinced of *your* true and devoted love, she will offer the same in return.

LOVE MEANS ALWAYS HAVING TO SAY YOU'RE SORRY

MOST OF US RELATE much more to a cat. Cats are very discerning lovers. They form friendships cautiously and expect give and take. The cat is secure with who she is. In touch with her feelings. Open . . . honest . . . free! Mind you, this is not always easy to live with. Cats aren't for the ego-fragile. Yet within the cat lies a pure, deep desire to become your intimate friend. Cats often appear ambivalent about how much love and attention they get, but do not be fooled. Every move of yours is observed and weighed by the cat. She's constantly looking for any indication that you just adore her.

D OGS ARE MORE PREDICTABLE than cats. With few exceptions, you know what a dog will do because you've trained it to do so. They work hard to perform according to your expectations. Though playful and full of boundless energy, most dogs remain domesticated. Not true for cats. Cats are, at the same time, an exotic wild animal and a demure little kitten-child. Your cat switches between these two mindsets several times per day! Cat-lovers find this fascinating — if not a bit unsettling.

Living with a cat is like sharing your home with a wild animal. Accepting this fact will ease your tension as kitty performs and displays her felineness. Your cat demonstrates daily her amazing hunting skills and sensory capabilities. Kitty becomes an exquisite hunter of that fly in the kitchen or that mouse or grasshopper just outside the door. And it may cause you to shudder, but those precision killing bites she inflicts on her poor prey are nothing short of masterful.

A cat's ears perk and twist around at sounds that reach your ears whole seconds later, if at all. Kitty will suddenly tear around the house at seemingly nothing. One moment she lies serenely curled in your lap and the next she is insisting on patrolling her territory. Just when you think you could practically rock that babe in your arms, kitty has trans-formed into a self-sufficient adult-type who has little need for you . . . for a while anyway!

"Kitty becomes an exquisite hunter of that fly in the kitchen or that mouse or grasshopper just outside the door."

A Priceless Work of Art

EVEN THE SMALLEST FELINE is a masterpiece," said Leonardo Da Vinci, whose works of art show off cats beautifully. See them in his paintings sleuthing about, playing like gymnasts or posing almost sensually. Not surprisingly, cats are likened to ballet dancers. Watch a cat walk, balanced effortlessly, along a narrow ledge or run flawlessly across the grass, or take a daring leap and make a silent, perfect landing. You are witnessing the ultimate in gracefulness. Remember this the next time you find your cat on top of your refrigerator or tip-toeing amongst the breakables on that shelf! Be overcome with awe at kitty's dexterity and light sure-footedness. Give him a break . . . he's being a marvelous specimen of cat.

". . . take a daring leap and make a silent, perfect landing."

CHAPTER TWO

Three Big Myths about Cats

B Y DEFINITION, A MYTH is a legendary belief that explains only part of the real story, and that is certainly the case with the three following cat myths. For example, cats do sleep and relax a lot, yet they are far from lazy. Also, cats are often coy and cautious when expressing affection, but they are certainly not unaffectionate. And finally, while a cat usually cannot be trained to perform upon command, you may be surprised what it *can* be trained to do.

MYTH 1
CATS ARE LAZY

Compared to dogs, most cats seem incredibly lazy! The picture that usually comes to mind when one says "cat" is a perfectly still feline, half-asleep, basking in the warmth of the sun or a favorite cozy chair. He lifts one eyelid as you whiz past, and you wonder just how much sleep this cat really needs.

At Least Twelve Hours of Sleep Per Day

ACTUALLY, CATS NEED ABOUT twelve hours of sleep per day. (Many older cats or less healthy cats require more like sixteen hours per day.) Hey, it's hard work being a cat! Many cat owners just assume their cats sleep virtually all day and all night because kitty is asleep during the day and *they* are asleep at night. The truth is, cats have wild parties and important meetings during the night when we humans are completely unaware.

Unlike dogs, cats are nocturnal animals. They naturally sleep by day and hunt by night. These odd sleeping patterns can be modified, but only slightly and only occasionally. Good luck.

The Boredom Question

SOMETIMES A PERFECTLY HEALTHY cat will sleep too much if it's bored. Even ten or fifteen minutes per day of human-initiated kitty workout time will help your cat get more exercise and sleep less. Involving the cat more in your life keeps boredom down, too.

During a cat's waking hours, one might mistake its slow approach to life as laziness. Look again. Cats accomplish what they want and need in a typical day, yet know instinctively how to pace themselves. A cat will not be rushed! Kitty will only exert herself when she's fully rested. This is partly why it's relaxing to be around a cat.

Dogs, on the other hand, never seem to tire of chasing and being chased. Most dog owners wear out long before the ever-ready dog. It is good that dogs join sled teams and not cats. The typical cat will not hesitate to abruptly stop playing or running when they become tired. But just as suddenly, a cat will fly into action — deciding that it immediately wants or needs to play.

On Exercise

CATS REQUIRE AND DESIRE completely different exercises than dogs, and cats usually get most of what they need all by themselves. A dog needs his owner to take him for a walk. Most cats figure out what they need and do it themselves. Even a totally indoor cat will often run around the house until he gets his heart racing and his muscles burning. It does help immensely though, if *you* become a playmate and provide toys, props and encouragement. You may get a decent workout too, if you keep pulling that string around the house.

MYTH 2
CATS ARE UNAFFECTIONATE

Warning: this next statement may be hazardous to your self-image. If your cat is unaffectionate, *you* may be unaffectionate. Not to say that kitty caused you to be that way. You may, however, have caused *kitty* to be that way. Your kitty could be starving for the essential hugs and kisses it needs.

MAKE THE FIRST MOVE

OF COURSE IT'S MORE than hugs and kisses. It's talking to kitty and inviting her to join you as you go about your day. It's stroking her fur and rubbing your cheek against hers and a whole lot more. Your cat will get her cue for affection from *you*. You get to show her how much affection is appreciated — and even expected — in your household! A cat at any age will respond to your attention, yet it's most effective when kitty is still a kitten and beginning to establish her patterns of needs and desires for human contact and involvement.

After a while, kitty will be oozing with demonstrative love. A cat won't be all over you like a dog, but it will caress you with more subtle expressions of fondness. Every gesture is completely sincere and deeply heartfelt. Cats are incapable of simply appearing to like you; what you see is what you get.

KITTY KISSES

KITTY KISSES ARE THE most coveted expressions of love. There are a few different ways that cats kiss. Some actually lick your cheek with their sandpapery tongue. More often, a cat will rub its mouth and nose and cheeks against your mouth and nose and cheeks. Besides the sheer coziness this gesture provides, the rubbing also allows for scent exchange between kitty and his human friend. Your cat wants your unique scent and his unique scent to mingle and create one big unique scent. The more your cat rubs you, the more he likes you . . . or wants you to like him.

Cats also kiss with their eyes. Haven't you ever had a cat look straight at you, then slowly close both eyes and then slowly open them again? Kitty may just be sleepy, but most often he's giving you a great big kitty kiss! You can always give one back, too. (It can get mushy.)

A KITTY PAT

HAVE YOU EVER HAD a cat pat your face? This is truly a sweet thing. They try to be ever-so-delicate. Usually this happens when kitty is lying on your lap or curled up on your chest as you recline. She stretches out her paw and reaches for your chin or cheek or forehead. It's a pat, pat, pat in slow motion, with accompanying purring. Sometimes the claws just barely dig in, but kitty means no harm.

LEG-WEAVING

FELINES ARE FAMOUS FOR weaving through our legs as we're standing. Cats especially love doing this in the kitchen as we are attempting to prepare food. (Perhaps they figure it's one place we're bound to stay for a while.) Although it can be an attention-getting device, twining around human legs is also a cat's way of saying, "I like you." If you're not best friends already, you've at least given him reason to believe that a friendship is possible. Besides bumping into you with his head, kitty's tail is also affectionately depositing his special scent on you as the tail winds around and around.

COUNTLESS EXPRESSIONS OF LOVE

CATS SHOW THEIR LOVE all day long in numerous ways. They often sleep near (or on) their beloveds. They melt into our laps for their daily fix. Sometimes it's just enough to be near us. Many cats will sit and stare . . . taking in every nuance of its human friends.

Having a cat fall in love with you and demonstrating affection in this way isn't a given — your friendship must be cultivated! Given a bit of time and a lot of patience your feline friend will *choose* you . . . and you will know it.

Once your cat has become accustomed to a lot of affection in your home, he may remind you of his need for it! If you haven't been paying enough attention to kitty, you may be attacked by your warm, weighty, purring fur ball — often in the wee hours of the morning when you aren't ready to get up. Or kitty may meow softly from a few yards away as if to say, "come over here and see me . . . or invite me over there where you are." Watch for this and respond to your cat.

MIXED SIGNALS

ONCE IN A WHILE, kitty could surprise you (even shock you) by acting as though she is not at all glad to see you after you've been gone. Whether it's been two days or just two hours, kitty may decide to treat you with contempt! It may be a scornful look. He may turn his back. Worse yet, your feline friend could bat at you as you walk past. This is most unsettling, if you have an otherwise wonderful relationship with your cat. There is a good explanation for this behavior. Even though kitty seems to be saying, "I don't like you very much, so there!" . . . what he's really saying is, "I like you so much that it hurts when you aren't here." Kitty is punishing you for not staying right where he wants you. Take it as a supreme compliment and stop to give your cat a little attention before moving on to other things.

THE OTHER EXTREME

REMARKABLY, YOUR CAT MAY display the opposite response in a similar situation the next time. Sometimes a cat who has been left alone for a day or two, temporarily starved of affection, will often insist on hugs and kisses *first* before visiting the replenished food bowl. (Perhaps many a cat has been thrown plenty of little dry pellets into its bowl when it's his heart that is empty.)

MYTH 3
CATS ARE UNTRAINABLE

It is true. Cats cannot be trained to do just what you want them to do. While dogs may be trained to understand and perform, cats can only be trained to *understand*. The performing is entirely up to them. There is a vast difference here. Kitty will never become your robot. He will *always* do only what he or she wants to do. But the more you train a cat to understand what you're asking, the more likely kitty will respond. And don't forget the all-important key: as you gain his respect you will notice a greater willingness on his part to consider your requests — simply because you are friends.

A LITTLE TRAINING

It takes gentle, consistent repetition to train cats to understand what we're saying. Cats are amazingly intelligent. It can be easy to expect too much from cats, yet at the same time, far too little. They are capable of learning to recognize countless words and phrases. How fun it is to be able to say, "Are you hungry?" and hear kitty *meow* with a firm "yes" and walk over to the food bowl. Or to ask, "Wanna be brushed?" and have the cat come galloping up onto your lap. Cats seem to enjoy their ability to understand us and the sky's the limit as far as how many words and phrases they can comprehend.

CURBING POOR BEHAVIOR

If you're just beginning to train your cat, it probably won't work to calmly say, "No, kitty, don't jump onto the coffee table," or, "Kitty, please stop clawing the chair." It takes time and repetition for cats to distinguish between different phrases and tones of voice. Initially, cats learn to modify their behavior only by association. In other words, it must be demonstrated to kitty in living color that bad things happen when he or she behaves in certain ways. You can punish your cat, but only by using safe, proven methods of discipline that do not damage your cat's delicate psyche. Once association has worked its disciplinary magic, your words alone will often be enough to correct kitty.

ACCENTUATING THE GOOD

You must also use association for rewards and affirmation of desirable behaviors. For instance, you can train your cat to understand that when she comes when you call it, a savory treat awaits. Or she gets a neck massage. Or maybe she gets to watch her favorite television show on birds and squirrels. Think up creative ways to motivate your feline friend. Food rewards are okay, but you'd be surprised how often they quit working. A cat may repeat a desired behavior for days or even a couple weeks to receive her treat and then one day lose all interest. Just when you think you've got kitty figured out everything may change. Keep it interesting. Stay flexible. Have fun with your cat!

PART TWO

What a Cat Hates . . . What a Cat Loves

THIS SECTION IS REALLY *the heart of the book . . . the nitty-gritty, practical stuff that is going to make the difference in how your cat responds to you and whether or not kitty will become a true friend and responsible, pleasant and happy member of your household!*

Each major category begins with what a cat "hates" about the topic at hand, and finishes with what a cat "loves" about the same subject. Don't skip over the "hates" part. It may not be as inspiring to read as the "loves" sections, perhaps, but they are equally important. You could be mistreating your cat (in her eyes) and sincerely not realizing it. Once you're aware of what not *to do with a cat, you can have fun practicing the countless* right *things to do! These are the little secrets to immeasurable happiness for you and your cat.*

CHAPTER THREE

Is It Playtime Yet?

PLAYING WITH YOUR CAT can be wonderfully fun and mutually rewarding for you and your feline friend. Although your direct participation in various games and activities is not required each and every time, it will be important to get right in there and play now and then, to keep things interesting for kitty. As indicated in the next several pages, cats respond well to play sessions that stimulate their instinctive desire to hunt — but only when the cat gets to be the hunter. Don't even *think* of asking kitty to be the hunted one.

Try the activities mentioned here and don't give up if your cat seems unwilling to play or appears to be confused about the objective of it all. Be patient and faithfully provide opportunities, toys and an occasional play moment between you and your cat.

Cats HATE Rough Play

I T'S EASY TO FORGET that your cat is a cat (and not a puppy) and play too rough. You may have convinced yourself that your kitty actually likes it. Or perhaps you are hoping that kitty will learn to like it. Save the energy. Trying to toughen up your cat won't work; many have tried before you. Rough play is actually mishandling. Kitty will rebel against this . . . one way or another. Rebellion might include tearing up a certain piece of furniture or going wee-wee in the wrong place, or becoming unusually ornery toward you and others.

CATS **LOVE** GENTLE, LIVELY PLAY

CATS LOVE TO PLAY . . . and not just as little energetic kittens. Your adult cat needs to play also. If you don't invite her to play a couple times a day she may make up her own games . . . and you won't appreciate them. (Her games may involve drapes, dangly things, furniture, vases on shelves, etc.) Kitty playtime tones her muscles, keeps boredom down, takes weight off and sharpens her hunting skills. Actually, the *only* thing your cat is truly interested in about playtime is the hunting practice. All games should be designed to stimulate your cat's natural hunting instinct. Stalk . . . pounce . . . kill. It's time for Attack Kitty!

48

YOUR NEW KITTEN

Kittens deserve special mention here. When an energetic, playful, funny little kitten comes to live at your house it is easy to forget that behind kitty's tough, I've-got-the-world-by-its-tail exterior lies an extremely sensitive and impressionable feline. Instinctively, a kitten usually exhibits a fair amount of confidence and resiliency toward the creatures in his world, and too often kitty becomes the victim of rough play or handling. It can begin innocently enough, as you find great entertainment chasing your animated kitten about the house or pretending to be a bigger, more aggressive "playmate." Regardless of how much fun kitty *seems* to be having at the time, be aware that each movement of yours is recorded by kitty and becomes part of what he thinks of you (and other humans) as he grows up. Quite often, a disillusioned cat owner will lament how the one- or two-year-old kitty has turned feisty, only to learn that poor kitty is merely trying to defend himself against the kinds of behaviors the cat owner displayed when kitty was young.

Should children be among those caring for your kitten, it is especially important to observe their handling of the cat and educate them appropriately. Certainly, if you are given the wonderful and unique opportunity to nurture a kitten in your household, give kitty (and yourself) a healthy start and practice the principles of loving cat-rearing mentioned in this book.

Cats **HATE** to be Chased

DOGS LOVE IT, OF course. They see it as play and will beg just about anyone to join in the game. Cats feel extremely threatened by being chased. A cat who is being chased believes his pursuer is actually out to get him . . . the same way a mouse feels when the cat is after it. Chasing your cat in the least bit will cause him to fear you and he will either become cowardly or strike out against you.

Cats **LOVE** to Chase Things

PULL A PIECE OF string or ribbon or yarn across the floor or dangle it nearby. Start it and stop it like a real little critter would move. For more excitement, tie interesting things on the end like feathers or netting. Flip it up in the air to resemble a bird or bug. Kitty should have to work to get it, but don't try and outsmart him by making it too hard or he'll become discouraged and give up.

Cats **HATE** Wrestling

DOGS CAN RARELY GET enough of it . . . especially on their back and underside. Cats cringe every time you pet too hard or too fast or too much! Kitty may start avoiding all petting opportunities.

Wrestling a cat involves "rolling" or "jiggling" your cat on the floor as it lies in its most vulnerable position — on its back. Many cat wrestlers try to get kitty to scratch and bite, too. This is a good thing to do if you want your cat to hate you. And don't be fooled into thinking your cat is having any kind of fun doing this. The reason he doesn't run away is because he's terrified of you, and he figures he'll get beaten to a pulp if he does anything but sit and take it. Reserve wrestling for the dog — he loves it.

Cats **LOVE** Paper Bags and Boxes

PAPER BAGS ARE OFTEN suggested for kittens to play in and around, but adult cats think they're cool too. With an older, more experienced cat you may need to get a little more creative. Hide a toy in the bag. Or once kitty is inside, tap or scratch the outside of the bag with a pencil or something as if a critter is doing it. Beware — kitty will pounce and tear the bag.

Boxes are also terrific playthings for kitty. Cats love to investigate in, on and around the box. And it seems to them to be the most clever bonus that they can sharpen their claws on them, too. Great fun!

DO NOT CRUSH

CATS **LOVE** TOY MICE

NEVER UNDERESTIMATE THE TOY mouse! Most cats grow bored with their fake little mice because nobody makes the mouse *do* anything. You've got to make it fly through the air and get stuck certain places and show up where kitty is least expecting it. Push it along the floor right in front of kitty's nose. Dangle it from somewhere. Dust off those forgotten mice and make them come alive!

CATS **HATE** TO BE TEASED

IT'S DIFFICULT TO PERSUADE dog lovers of this, because dogs seem to thrive on it. But to a cat, teasing is dumb. Not to mention bewildering and upsetting. Teasing is a concept that cats do not fathom. Favorite forms of teasing include making aggressive, attack-like sounds or lunging at kitty. Your cat will come to view you as "The Household Enemy." Mimicking or making fun of kitty in his presence will also undermine your relationship severely. Cats don't belittle us and they are puzzled that we would do such a thing to them.

Also, never start to play with kitty and then tease him by not actually following through and playing. Besides disappointing your feline friend, you are planting the seeds of distrust and when you are finally ready to play, kitty may have lost interest *and* trust.

*"Cats don't belittle us and they are puzzled
that we would do such a thing to them."*

Cats LOVE the Pencils & Pens Game

SIMPLY LINE UP TEN or twenty pens and/or pencils on your kitchen counter (or other table surface) and let kitty knock them off one by one from her perch on a nearby chair or stool. At first, you may need to partially hide them under some junk mail and get the game going. Keep this game limited to one spot in your home, or kitty may think that all small items on the edges of tables are meant to fall to the floor.

Cats LOVE to Play Hide-and-Seek

THIS IS A GREAT game for kitty. The idea is to move a small object (ball, coin, toy mouse, large button, etc.) under a newspaper or small rug as if it is alive under there. Kitty will investigate and stalk and pounce at it. Be careful of your hand if kitty has claws . . . you may need gloves!

Cats **LOVE** to Play Soccer

FIND A SMALL BALL or disc that skims really well across your vinyl or hardwood floors. Things that work nicely are buttons, large beads or a waded up piece of aluminum foil. The idea is to position yourself at least six feet from kitty and kick (with your hand or foot) the object past him. Once kitty gets the hang of this, he'll stop the "ball" and may even kick it back to you. Build the tension by pretending to kick it a few times (warming up) before you actually do . . . cats love the suspense.

Cats **HATE** to be Laughed At

IF YOUR CAT DOES something that makes him or her look silly, foolish or clumsy, it is very important that you refrain from laughing. Cats need to hang onto their dignity or they're likely to become depressed or develop a complex and behave strangely. When kitty falls or knocks something over accidentally, try to look away or pretend you didn't even notice. (Kitty will act as if she didn't do it, in order to try and save face).

Cats **LOVE** Catnip

CATNIP IS AN HERB from the mint family that most cats flip over. It's really a drug for kitties! Lucky for them, the specific oil found in catnip, *hepetalactone*, is not harmful to cats and leaves no ill side effects. Kitty slowly begins licking the catnip, then chews at it wildly. Soon he will be rubbing it all over his cheeks and chin. By now kitty is euphoric. While cats find catnip entrancing, they aren't exactly addicted. Usually, a cat will take a catnip "trip" every few days, for about five to ten minutes at a time, but if catnip is not around they don't seem to miss it.

CHAPTER FOUR

How to Say No! (and Yes!)

E VEN AS THE RELATIONSHIP between you and your cat begins to transform, kitty will still act in ways that are simply unacceptable in your home (a reality that will never be completely eradicated, because a cat will always do certain cat things), and it's going to be necessary to discourage these less-than-perfect behaviors as best you can. To aid you in your efforts, this chapter offers a look at a few golden rules in the realm of cat discipline and behavior modification that are very simple and easily carried out. This is important stuff to learn — and often the pivotal place in cat and human relations where the most trust and respect are built. Take the time to understand the feline psyche and discover how to healthily motivate your cat.

Cats HATE Obedience Training

THE CONCEPT OF OBEDIENCE is pretty much meaningless to cats. You can't even find the word in their dictionary! Cats loathe anything that smells of training. Trying to bully or frighten a cat into doing *anything* is going to backfire. It may be hazardous to your health and sanity . . . and certainly puts your relationship with kitty in jeopardy.

Besides the obvious, like being forced to come or stay or jump down or go to their room . . . cats hate being forced to sit on your lap or go outside or eat their dinner or stop meowing or just about anything. And they definitely resent being forced to smile for the camera!

CATS LOVE LITTLE REWARDS

CATS REMEMBER THE TREATS. If you are trying to reinforce a good behavior — such as (eventually) coming in from the outside when called — be sure to have a kitty treat waiting (any grocery store has special goodies just for cats). It won't always work, but it will help. Reward her often even after she has developed the good habit, to help her associate her actions with pleasure. Try to save rewards for the behaviors that really count in your household.

Cats **LOVE** Explanations

SOMETIMES KITTY JUST NEEDS a good talking-to. A good old fashioned this-is-why-that-was-wrong talk. People might think you're nuts — but this often works! Cats need to hear your slow, serious voice. Of course they won't catch all the words but they'll get the general idea. A thoughtful heart-to-heart combines the love they so desire and the firmness they need . . . to see that you really mean business.

Cats **HATE** to be Hit

NEVER, NEVER, NEVER, NEVER, *never*, hit a cat. This is absolutely non-negotiable! Resorting to hitting or swatting your cat will damage his psyche and kill his trust in you. Dogs respond to an appropriate swat at the right time and the right place. They are wired to accept it as training. Cats aren't. Cats will hold it against you . . . perhaps for life. And they won't be the better for it. So don't be cruel . . . be cool!

CATS **LOVE** PRAISE AND AFFIRMATION

K ITTY WILL SHOW AMAZING results if handled correctly. The trick is to modify behavior without breaking the delicate feline spirit. It can be done! You must create a loving, positive atmosphere in which your cat will enjoy improving herself.

You can't get enough praise and affirmation and neither can kitty. It won't hurt to over-do this. Cats need it desperately. It assures them of your love and approval. A cat is more likely to "do the right thing" if he associates the right thing with your oohs and aahs. Praise kitty even when it seems unnecessary or silly! Praise him profusely for scratching at the scratching post, showing up when you call him, hopping onto your lap or jumping down from the place he's not allowed.

Cats **HATE** Being Yelled At

THE GRUFF, AUTHORITATIVE VOICE that can be so effective with dogs wreaks havoc on a cat. Besides literally hurting their ultra-sensitive ears, your continued loud commands will break your cat's spirit. This is a sure way to alienate kitty and lose her respect.

Cats **LOVE** Mild Correction

THERE ARE THREE EXCELLENT methods for on-the-spot discipline. Since hitting a cat in any way is absolutely out of the question, you've got to get creative when kitty does a very bad thing like clawing the leather chair, deciding to snack on the thawing meat or taking a swipe at your face. The idea is to make kitty miserable without causing her to be scared of you. You are trying to get kitty to associate this misery with the wrong behavior. And the punishment must be delivered during the act or *immediately* after. Waiting any more than about 10 seconds is too long and will cause far more harm than good.

THE SHRIEK

Open your mouth and let out one short, loud, bone-chilling shriek right in kitty's ear. It must be short and it must be LOUD. You can either just shriek or yell a word, like, "NO!" or "STOP!" or "HEY!". Kitty should definitely stop doing whatever it is she's doing. This works from across the room as well as right next to your cat.

If your cat starts biting or clawing your hand during petting, brushing, playing or any other time for any reason, you *must* resist the intense urge to pull your hand away. Taking your hand away when your cat is acting this aggressively will only make her think that *she* can rule over you! As strange as it seems, if you leave your hand there and shout "NO!" very, very loudly, kitty will let go . . . and gain enormous respect for you. In time, your cat will strike out less and less and when she does, you may receive a sweet, sorrowful rub of apology when she realizes how she hurt you.

THE BLOW

This method is only effective at short range. You simply blow hard right into kitty's face. The sensation is enough to halt her and kitty will be taken aback. But don't keep doing it after the initial blow. One good blast should do it.

THE SPRAY BOTTLE

Don't live without it! This works wonderfully. It's worth having a couple of spray bottles around the house. When kitty does something undesirable, just spray him with the water (in the face is the best, but not too forcefully). Cats hate the sensation. Once kitty stops misbehaving, stop the spraying.

CHAPTER FIVE

All in the Family

CATS CONSIDER THEMSELVES TO be actual members of their human family, whether their human companions treat them like one of the gang or not. You can understand why, then, that a cat who feels left out of the affairs of the family might become depressed or discouraged. It's not always easy to spot this condition in kitty, and if your household rushes through most weeks at high speed, the cat may get lost in the shuffle. In this chapter, you will be made aware of some commonly overlooked feline preferences which just may cause you to say, "Wow, I didn't realize that." Assume that the following assertions are true and watch what happens with your kitty when you seek to include her in your daily routines.

Cats **HATE** Being Ignored or Excluded

MOST CAT OWNERS ARE surprised to learn that cats are *not* the extreme loners they are said to be. This is not a concept we are used to hearing, and it takes a while to alter our thinking. A feline will *somewhat* adjust to an owner who pretty much leaves him alone, but he certainly does not prefer it! Often, cats who feel excluded will turn resentful. You may not realize that your cat is secretly longing for more attention and interaction. That contented-looking blob on the chair is possibly not as happy as he looks — and can't wait to be included in the family!

Cats **HATE** Being Left Alone

PEOPLE OFTEN SAY: "I'LL get a cat for a pet, because I'm gone all day and a cat won't mind that." Hah! Have you ever asked a cat? This is a great misconception. While it is correct that cats are handy to leave alone as far as the litter box is concerned, there is no truth to the assertion that cats miss their human companions any less than dogs would miss theirs. Believing this falsehood could lead to leaving your cat behind much, much more than is healthy.

Of course cats can be left alone during the workday and, if *absolutely* necessary, for up to 48 hours, provided they have food, water and a litter box. If you go away for longer, ask a cat-loving neighbor to spend a few minutes a day with kitty — it will make a huge difference! Better yet, find a housesitter to stay with kitty for the duration of your trip.

Leaving a cat completely alone longer than a couple days is really hard on kitty, and he or she *will* suffer. Even after a normal workday alone, a cat needs to be given quality kitty-time. Cats can easily feel abandoned when their human companions run off and leave them. Sometimes they're just too proud to show it!

CATS **LOVE** BEING INCLUDED IN THE FAMILY

I T'S ACTUALLY GREAT FUN getting kitty involved in all kinds of unexpected ways. This is not hard work. Little changes in how you view your cat will translate into treating kitty as an important member of your family. Your cat will love you for it!

Let kitty know that she is invited to follow you around the house as you move about your day. Specifically invite her to come into the kitchen and watch you prepare dinner . . . or let her know she's welcome at the computer or while reading the newspaper. Perhaps you wouldn't mind a little company while putting on your make-up in the morning or drinking your cup of coffee.

The point is, most cats are amused by watching us . . . but they must first feel *invited* to join us; sometimes over and over. Include kitty in your day and soon little routines and rituals will form. You may soon miss your cat's company when she skips a day or two for whatever reason.

Cats LOVE Chit-Chat

I T ISN'T NECESSARY TO carry on a continual dribble of conversation with your cat, but don't hold back the kind of typical chit-chatting you would do with a human housemate. Cats like this . . . they really do. Always make a point to warn kitty when you're about to leave the house or go to bed. Be courteous and kind. Cats who enjoy a loving, stimulating relationship with their owners appreciate some lead time to prepare for being apart from their beloveds.

Acknowledge your cat's presence with a "Hi, _____"(your cat's name) several times throughout the day. Cats thrill to know that you are aware of them and that you're glad they're there. If you're trying to encourage kitty to come see what you're doing, keep asking, "here kitty, come here . . . c'mon kitty," and repeat it. At first, if your cat is not used to this, it may seem puzzled. But don't give up. In time, your kitty will wonder what's wrong with you when you're unusually quiet.

Cats HATE Being "On Display"

C ATS APPEAR AS OBJECTS of art in many ways, but they dislike being treated as something inanimate. A cat loves feeling attractive and it will naturally spend a fair amount of time just sitting there looking beautiful, but cats want more from life than that! Your cat may be picking up on the fact that she is not regarded as the capable, intelligent creature she truly is.

How often do you speak to your cat? Do you talk to your cat only when it needs to be disciplined? Only when kitty deserves praise? Are you mostly silent the rest of the time? Kitty hears everyone talking to everyone else all the time. She wonders if she is invisible or something! She fears that the humans in her life may *never* converse with her.

CATS **LOVE** TO LEARN HUMAN WORDS

CATS ARE INTELLIGENT, AND it is no more apparent than when teaching them to understand our words. Your cat will get a kick out of learning to recognize certain words and phrases. By repeating something like "wanna go outside?" and following it up with going to the door and starting to open it, you are reinforcing what you just said. Once outside with kitty, you can repeat the word "outside," which will help her attach the right meaning to the word. Repeating and associating works with just about anything. Try teaching kitty to recognize "Are you hungry?", "Milk?", "Do you want a kitty-treat?", "Tuna!", "Wanna be brushed?", or "Look! There's a birdie/bug/squirrel!" Be patient and have fun . . . you'll be amazed.

Cats can also learn to comprehend things we say that don't require an "answer" from them. For instance, to make kitty feel better, you can reassure him when you leave the house by saying "I'll be back soon." Or you can say comforting words when she is scared; perhaps, "It's okay kitty." It works like a charm. The tried and true "good kitty!" still communicates to kitty that you're pleased with her.

*"Cats thrill to know that you are aware of them
and that you're glad they're there."*

CATS **HATE** BEING BANNED FROM PLACES

COMMON SENSE TELLS YOU that you shouldn't let kitty explore the dryer, dishwasher or a hot burner, etc. Yet there are other interesting places that may seem like they should be off-limits but are really not a problem. The bathroom faucet is a good example. A trickling faucet provides much needed drinking water and is a fascination to many kitties. Or, you might consider letting your cat wander through a particular cupboard that's usually closed. Cats also appreciate having the pick of the furniture for curling up on; and if kitty's been brushed and is flea-free he shouldn't damage a thing.

CATS **HATE** TO BE SHUT IN A ROOM

YOUNG KITTENS OFTEN NEED to be corralled into a room when they are learning about litter boxes, clawing and other feline members of the household. Occasionally an adult cat should be placed briefly and temporarily in a protected room during especially disruptive home repairs or remodels. But beyond that, it is considered punishment to shut a cat into a room. (If discipline is what's needed, there are other effective ways.) Shutting out kitty from the family and the rest of the house is the opposite of what kitty needs and desires. You will make him or her very angry and lose ground in your attempt to raise a happy, well-adjusted cat.

CATS **LOVE** THE RUN OF THE HOUSE

I F YOUR CAT IS strictly indoors, it's good to give him or her access to pretty much everywhere. Cats are curious and love to investigate their surroundings continually. Keep doors open that you normally would. Now and then, let kitty explore a closet or cupboard. It seems to be a real treat, for most cats, to curl up in someone's soft underwear drawer once in a while — and it really won't hurt anything (provided you check for flea infestation on kitty, first). Cats naturally explore, as part of their hunting instinct. While it isn't advisable to allow kitty onto kitchen counters, eating tables or inside china hutches, try not to restrict kitty from other high places. Window sills, book shelves, entertainment centers, dressers and closet shelves are favorite high-up hangouts.

Also, you or one of the kids might want to invite the cat onto the bed at night if both parties involved don't mind. Sleep like you usually do; most cats will get used to the tossing and turning that goes on around and under them. If not, that's okay too. At least kitty will know she's been welcomed.

CHAPTER FIVE All in the Family

CATS **LOVE** A PLACE AT THE TABLE

A ND ON THE BED. And in the middle of your exercise routine. And just about anywhere else his favorite humans are hanging out! (And you thought cats were loners.) Your dear cat would probably jump for joy if you pulled out a chair for him at the table and invited him up. Don't feed him there but he can certainly enjoy the lively dinner conversation. Try saving out a tiny tidbit of dinner and show him that you're keeping it just for him. After dinner, make a ritual out of taking the food-token to his dish on the floor.

CATS **LOVE** A SIP OF MILK NOW AND THEN

M OST CATS ABSOLUTELY LOVE milk, but you should never give it to your kitty in excess. A couple teaspoons per day is enough to treat your cat without causing diarrhea or gas (stop, if kitty develops this). If kitty doesn't tolerate straight milk well, try substituting with a dot of yogurt or cottage cheese. Dairy products are a good source of vitamin A and much needed moisture in a cat's diet . . . but definitely watch the amounts. You can think up fun ways to present the milk, too. Like always leaving a spoonful in the bottom of your cereal bowl or taking down a certain cup when it's time for kitty's milk treat.

CHAPTER SIX

Those Feline Habits

WHILE MOST CATS ARE fastidious about grooming and completely capable of taking good care of themselves, it is unrealistic to think that your kitty doesn't need your direction or intervention on occasion and the benefit of your growing knowledge of cats. If you have chosen to keep a cat for a pet, it is within your job description to see to it that your kitty remains in the best of mental and physical health. The next few pages provide a look at how your cat may need your assistance in reaching that famous feline state of utter contentment.

Cats HATE Losing Their Physique

CATS LIKE TO BE well-groomed, healthy and fit. They desperately need a healthy self-image in order to stay in a good mood! Kitty may withdraw, turn cranky or dabble in mischief if she feels poorly about herself. As a cat owner, you have the responsibility of helping your cat maintain his highly valued physique and the skills he depends on.

Cats LOVE Exercising Their Instincts

CATS ARE DELIGHTED TO be cats . . . they really are. Life is good when kitty can jump, run, climb, claw, hunt, groom and sleep. A cat knows when it's in proper physical shape; his mood is brighter, his activity varied and more intense. The goal is to help kitty stay healthy, maintain his wonderful physique and sharpen his marvelous skills. Much of a cat's care can be easily done by kitty himself. Now and then you will need to do some hands-on care. Often, you get the privilege of playing coach and trainer with that furry ballet dancer of yours.

CATS **HATE** HAVING FLEAS

THE PROBLEM OF FLEAS annoys cats and cat owners alike. Cats who scratch themselves often throughout the day may be suffering from an infestation. It is unkind to not come to the aid of a flea-fighting feline. They are most miserable creatures when a flea population has gained the upper hand. The painful flea bites, itching and general unbelievable frustration affects their sleep, moods and exercise. Most cats also bite at the fleas. Inevitably, a cat will then swallow a flea that is carrying some kind of an intestinal parasite (worms) and a whole new problem arises for kitty.

Cats LOVE to be Free of Fleas

IF YOUR CAT HAS fleas, do him a big favor and wage war against the little blood-sucking twerps. There are several good products on the market. Quite effective are the crystals that get sprinkled over your carpets and upholstery. Chemical house sprays work well too. Also, check with your veterinarian about the relatively new pill for cats that works on fleas from the inside out.

Treat your home instead of gooping up kitty with powders or sprays. (Flea collars help some, but don't get real high marks.) Flea dips and flea baths strip kitty of the fleas as well as her precious natural oils . . . and if you haven't treated your home, the hungry fleas will be waiting for your cat when she returns. Flea combs are useful for trapping a flea or two right off kitty as well as determining just how bad the flea problem is. As you're flea-combing kitty, keep a jar of hot water nearby and drown the fleas as you find them — before they have a chance to escape. Fleas leave behind "flea dirt" (their excrement: your cat's blood) and a flea comb will also pick that up. If lots of tiny black specks appear, you know you've got problems.

Cats **HATE** Getting De-clawed

THERE IS LITTLE DEBATE among the experts; removing a cat's primary means of defense should be considered the absolute last resort. Most cat owners turn to de-clawing kitty after enough furniture is ruined or faces are scratched. To be perfectly blunt, the course of action for a clawing cat is *not* de-clawing. Rarely are *all* other solutions explored by frustrated cat owners . . . such as better nurturing and diligent, loving re-training. Rendering your cat defenseless will stop him or her from clawing, but you will most always end up with a cat who feels maimed, unworthy, ashamed and weak; and his personality is likely to change. It would be a far better plan to re-train kitty.

CATS **LOVE** TO SHARPEN THEIR CLAWS

IF YOU TRIM YOUR cat's claws, you may have noticed that he or she scratches at things all the more. This is normal. Kitty must quickly sharpen the claws that you made short and dull. A cat's claws are its best defense against larger animals and its most prized hunting tool, and cats will instinctively sharpen them. The goal is razor-sharp; able to cleanly pierce bug, mouse or enemy with one perfect swipe. To keep them sharp as needles, kitty must scratch at something several times per day.

Well-trained and lovingly nurtured cats should mostly claw only where you want them to. It is not enough, however, to merely outlaw clawing the furniture. You must provide him or her with a high-quality scratching post. Many cat owners have lost faith in the effectiveness of scratching posts . . . but it's usually the homemade posts that are the problem. Homemade scratching posts are often not built sturdy enough to support the full weight of an adult cat who is furiously clawing. Go ahead and build one if you like, but build it strong enough. A good rule of thumb: the post needs to have at least a 4-inch diameter and the base should be at least a 16-inch diameter square. The post itself should be at least 22 inches high. Kitty will refuse his scratching post if he doubts for a moment that it will support him. A good pet store will have lots of posts to choose from, and a super-deluxe one is worth every penny!

Once outside, kitty has her pick of trees and stumps for sharpening those amazing claws. Sometimes cats will use a fence, old boards or a doormat. And there's a bonus: if your cat spends any amount of time outdoors, you probably won't need to trim her claws. All the rough surfaces outdoors naturally trim her claws a little at a time. So Kitty won't be as obsessed with sharpening her claws indoors if she visits the great outdoors most every day. Only a full-time indoor cat will grow super-long claws that you would need to trim. When kitty's claws get long, be sure to clip them before they start to irritatingly snag everything kitty comes in contact with. Your cat's vet can demonstrate to you the fine art of claw trimming.

Cats **LOVE** to Visit the Outdoors

YOUR CAT WOULD PROBABLY love to spend most of its time outside if the decision was left up to him, but you need to juggle his wishes and your knowledge of the big bad dangers out there. Cats love the outdoors because it's the world they were created for. Trees are perfect for climbing and spying . . . and great for sharpening claws. Summer lawns provide endless hunting practice sessions with gnats, moths and other flying things. A number one kitty pastime is people/squirrel/bird watching, and the outside is loaded with opportunities. And cats love to breathe fresh air and bask in the warm sun just like you do!

One of the main reasons your cat wants to go outside is to patrol and "mark" his or her territory. It's instinctive. (Your cat marks her indoor territory by rubbing on furniture and walls and by using a litter box.) Kitty can *view* the outdoor world through a window, but only an occasional romp outside will completely satisfy her urge to claim some of the land as her own. Going potty outside at certain spots around the edges of a cat's territory is the feline way of saying, "This is my land, and I'm the Queen here!" Multiple cats in the neighborhood make this very interesting, but they often work it out and settle for smaller or joint territories.

*"Kitty can **view** the outdoor world through a window, but only an occasional romp outside will completely satisfy her urge to claim some of the land as her own."*

INDOOR VS. OUTDOOR CAT

To simply decree that your cat will be a completely indoor or outdoor cat may not be wise. Perhaps your cat deserves something in-between. Restricting kitty to a totally indoor life does seem rather cheerless, but leaving the schedule entirely up to kitty isn't the best solution either. It takes just a tiny bit more work to raise your kitty as an indoor cat with outside privileges, but it's worth it! The idea is for kitty to be outside just enough to be delighted and enriched by the whole experience, yet not spending so much time out there that she's in danger in any way.

FREE REIGN

So maybe you're confused. Why is it so wrong to give a cat free reign outside? Isn't the outdoors where it was meant to live? Yes, the feline was meant to live outside, but the "outside" of today is vastly different from the "outside" of generations ago, at least where most of us live. A free-roaming cat in the neighborhoods of today is in constant danger of being hit by a car, getting snatched by a coyote, contracting a disease, picking up excessive mites and fleas or being abused. We live in a busier, more crowded, more industrialized world and we need to protect these precious animals we bring into our particular corner of that world! Follow the guidelines below for how to give your cat the gift of the outdoors in a safe, responsible way. As always . . . your kitty will love you for it! The goal is to treat your cat to one or two brief, monitored outdoor excursions per day. Here are the guidelines:

1. Try to let kitty out at approximately same times each day. Avoid darkness (cats are prone to stray).

2. Stay out with kitty for the first few weeks/months.

3. Decide on the boundaries. Follow kitty around and let him know when he's crossed the line. Praise him for staying within the boundary!

4. Practice going back to the door and calling kitty to come in. Praise her for coming! Offer a tasty incentive when she returns

home. She will need to be rewarded *each time* . . . not always with something to eat, but definitely often enough to associate coming in with pleasure. It also helps to jingle a bell (high pitched) or set of keys to signal that it's time to come back.

5. Start with 5-minute sessions outside. Gradually work toward one or two 20-minute outdoor romps per day.

6. Don't give up . . . and don't punish him for not returning. *Always praise your cat for walking through that doorway!* (Who wants to come home and get punished?) Your cat should eventually respond to your call when time is up, if you've been patient with kitty all along and showering him with praise and a frequent reward. Unlike a dog, your cat probably won't come running; expect anywhere from a 1- to 10-minute response time. Kitty may even come home on his own after a while . . . but not consistently. Now and then, kitty will backslide and you'll simply need to go find him. A final note — be sure to set a timer if you're apt to forget that kitty is out!

Remember, your goal here is not absolute adherence to this plan; just keep in mind that you are providing your otherwise indoor cat with outdoor visits in a safe and sane manner. However you work out the fine details is between you and your feline friend.

USING A LEASH

Don't rule out leash training. Cats certainly won't take to it like dogs, but it's handy to train your cat to use a leash for unusual situations, such as going outside after dark or taking a little outdoor excursion at an unfamiliar place. Or, if you're not too excited about letting kitty roam outside by himself at all (and the extra work that careful monitoring does require), leash training can be a good compromise. You'll find that kitty's pace is very, very slow with many stops and starts . . . don't ever push or force him! Some cats truly like to walk on a leash, and if leash walking is your cat's only chance to visit the outdoors, he will eventually look forward to it and love you for it.

Cats **HATE** Matted Fur

A HEALTHY, FIT CAT WILL "comb" its entire furry coat at least once each day with its tongue. This ritual serves to clean and smooth the fur. A long-haired kitty needs extra help from a willing human, though, or thick mats of fur will develop, particularly on its underside. It's painful for kitty to have mats removed once they've formed, and it's no fun to have the vet cut them out either. Eeeks!

Cats **LOVE** Clean, Glossy Fur

THIS IS WHY YOU see cats licking their fur so often. What you are witnessing is an incredible obsession with staying clean. You can help your cat feel fabulous by brushing his coat at least once a week (more often if kitty goes outside or has long hair). Besides getting rid of some of the dirt, brushing removes loose hairs that kitty would otherwise swallow. These nasty hairs build up inside kitty and cause the dreaded Hair Ball; miserable for your cat and a yucky mess to clean up! Brushing and petting also bring out the oils in a cat's coat which give it that silky sheen.

Cats **HATE** to be Overfed

YOUR KITTY MAY SEEM to disagree with this. Most healthy cats just love mealtime and can begin a pattern of overeating if encouraged at all. While your cat might enjoy the act of eating, he hates what overfeeding does to him. A fat cat can't run and jump like he should. Too big of a belly can actually make it difficult or impossible for kitty to clean himself properly. Extra weight puts a strain on kitty's joints, bones and entire body. And worse yet, the life expectancy of an overweight cat is shortened.

If your cat has slowly gained weight, you may not realize that he or she is overweight. Optimally, you shouldn't be able to grab much flab at all on a cat's underside. Also note kitty's energy level and physical activ-

ity. If you're not sure if your particular cat is just "big-boned" or truly overweight, take her to the vet and find out. Follow doctor's orders strictly and remember that you're doing kitty a big favor.

There are many excellent, high quality cat foods on the market. You can find cat food for growing kittens, active adults, sedentary cats and cats with special medical challenges. Ask your cat's vet for suggestions and then follow the feeding instructions on the bag carefully. A common mistake is to feed kitty just a little too much, and think the small extra amount won't matter. Actually, a handful too much goes a long way for a kitty. Don't let kitty wrap you around its paw with his crying for more food, if you are providing him with the amount your vet advises. Once kitty trims down to a healthy weight, he will be satisfied with his meals. You won't have to feel guilty about giving your cat a treat now and then, either.

Cats **LOVE** to be Fed Healthy Meals

O F COURSE IF YOU asked one, he'd probably say "no." What cats don't know won't hurt them. When fed high-nutritional meals, a feline has the best chance for feeling and looking his best. And a healthy cat is definitely a happy cat! As stated previously, ask your vet for recommendations on which cat food to buy for your unique kitty and follow feeding directions carefully. The better cat foods cost more — there's just no getting around it. But the result will be a healthier, happier cat.

THE BASIC FEEDING GUIDELINES

It's a good idea to feed your cat twice a day, at about the same time each day. Kitty should not have to beg for her regular meals. Always provide plenty of fresh water for kitty to drink. (You'd be surprised how often a cat's water bowl is disgustingly dirty!) Keep variety in your cat's diet . . . ask your vet if there's any medical reason why your cat cannot tolerate an occasional canned food or alternate treat. If you introduce variety in kitty's diet when he is young, he's less likely to become finicky later on.

*" . . . feel free to give kitty a treat
now and then of some raw egg,
a bit of lightly cooked meat or fish
and even a dot of cooked vegetables."*

GIVING YOUR CAT TREATS

It is great fun to watch one's cat thoroughly delighting in a surprise treat! Store-bought goodies are fine in moderation, but don't rely on them. Unless your cat has a particular intolerance (always ask your vet for advice and watch for signs of distress) you should feel free to give kitty a treat now and then of some raw egg, a bit of lightly cooked meat or fish and even a dot of cooked vegetables. Very small amounts of dairy products are usually received well, too. The main objective here is to supplement your cat's diet with a little excitement.

CHAPTER SEVEN

Affection With a Capital "A"

THIS LAST CHAPTER MAY well contain one of the keys to unprecedented happiness for you and your beloved feline friend. Nothing short of sheer joy and pure fun are in store for the cat owner who decides to win kitty's heart. Cats of course, are notorious for masking their true feelings when it comes to human affection, but once they've been found out . . . it is just a matter of time before kitty's protective front melts and a sensitive, loving, vulnerable feline emerges. Just to alert you: it's very possible that you will fall head-over-heels in love with that soft, warm, emotional little cat-creature of yours. Read on and enjoy practicing your cat's language; kitty won't mind your awkward start, and — don't worry — she isn't expecting fluency just yet.

CATS HATE WHEN HUMANS ARE TOO BUSY

HOW OFTEN HAVE YOU heard it said that cats are aloof? Cats are not naturally aloof but many cats *become* aloof from owners who are aloof because they think cats are aloof! It's nutty. Someone started this rumor long ago and we've been suffering the consequences ever since.

Cats can sense when they're being squished out of our lives. It's hard enough on them when we insist on this nasty habit of going off to work, let alone the agonizing loneliness they feel when people *are* home but not paying much attention to them! The absolute bare minimum amount of undivided attention a cat needs from a significant human per day is twenty minutes. You might be thinking, "Oh dear, my family barely gets that much time on some days!" Just remember that your cat will indeed suffer if the affection you hold for her is not expressed deliberately and meaningfully each and every day.

"Cats actually do crave the deep, committed, I'm-in-this-for-the-long-haul kind of love that a human companion can offer."

CATS **LOVE** TO BE LOVED

A FEW CAT OWNERS IN this world would like to debate this . . . but it is absolutely true. Cats actually do *crave* the deep, committed, I'm-in-this-for-the-long-haul kind of love that a human companion can offer. They only appear to have a take-it-or-leave-it attitude. Begin loving your cat in a language she can understand and kitty will feel safe enough to love you back. Once you've entered into an intimate friendship with a feline, it's much like signing a pact. You will have won kitty's heart and she will respect you profoundly. And this is one high-maintenance relationship that is definitely worth the investment. Now go find that kitty of yours!

Cats **HATE** It When Owners are Aloof

AN ALOOF CAT WHO lives with aloof humans probably spends hours pondering why his human friends act so strangely toward him . . . as if he were a piece of sculpture or a painting on the wall or simply a cat who *wants* to be left alone all the time. And because cats are rather insecure creatures when it comes to truly believing that we love and adore them, it is the rare cat who will possess the courage to tell us how wrong we are about some of our notions about cats. But they would if they could! Most often, however, cats adopt an "oh well" attitude and just plug along in life being grossly misunderstood.

Cats **LOVE** to Hear Their Names

HUMANS LIKE TO HEAR their names spoken and so does the feline population. But cats need to hear their names even *more* than people do! Kitty understands relatively few of our human words, so we need to emphasize the ones she does recognize. A name is totally unique, and a cat seems to know it.

Always say kitty's name while doing pleasant things with her like petting, brushing (if she likes it), massaging, etc. Avoid using kitty's name too often when disciplining or asking it to stop misbehaving. Kitty will associate her name with whatever is happening at the time she hears it. Besides feeling good all over from hearing her name, you will find that kitty will more often come when she's called, because she connects her name with nice things happening.

Cats **LOVE** to Hear Mushy Talk

A CAT WON'T UNDERSTAND MOST of our words, but kitty will catch the essence of what we're saying. He loves to hear that you missed him, or that he's handsome, or that he's the most wonderful cat in the world, or that he's a very good fly-hunter, etc. Cats like it when you say "goodnight" and "good morning" in earnest. They appreciate a little tenderness when you are about to leave and a little fussing over when you return. The little phrases that make life sweeter for your child, spouse or parent are what we're talking about here. Love your kitty with words and you may hear a few back from him in his own special way.

Cats LOVE A Warm Lap

THIS SHOULD BE SO obvious! We all know that one of a cat's most favorite places to spend time is curled up on a warm, cozy lap . . . but how often do we actually provide one for kitty?

Once you've plopped down somewhere for a while, be sure to specifically *invite* your cat to come onto your lap. He won't always need an invitation of course, but now and then he will need reassurance that he's welcome. Try not to move around a lot and break it to him gently when you need to get up.

Cats HATE to Beg for Attention

IT'S TRUE THAT MOST cats get somewhat used to not getting enough attention, but these cats are still not happy-as-can-be and they aren't too proud to explode with the resentment that's been building up! A cat may claw a known no-no spot, swipe at you as you walk by, stay outside way too long, dig up a plant, knock over a vase of flowers and create a waterfall or go wee-wee on the bed or carpet. (Just because a cat does these naughty acts doesn't necessarily mean you're not paying enough attention to it; it may be receiving the *wrong* kind of attention.)

CATS **LOVE** PETTING & STROKING

PETTING IS POSITIVELY MESMERIZING to a cat and very relaxing for the human doing the petting; it's one of the best things you can do with your feline friend. It is probably not a surprise that cats love to be petted. But have you been petting your cat the wrong way? Dogs enjoy a more vigorous petting, complete with a wild scratching session and an occasional pat on the head, back or tummy. For kitty, this kind of petting would cross the line to rough play.

Cats like to be petted slow, easy and thorough. Use your whole hand and stroke kitty with long, smooth motions. Do several head-to-tail strokes and allow plenty of time for kitty's favorite spots. Most cats will gladly indulge in being petted on their cheeks, chin, top of head and neck. Your cat is unusual if it likes its tummy or legs touched much at all. As for scratching, kitty should love to be tenderly scratched on his cheeks, chin and perhaps top of head.

KNOW WHEN TO STOP (OR START)

With dogs, it's easy to figure out whether or not they are in the mood to be petted. The answer is usually, "YES! I AM!" And the answers to how often and how much? You guessed it: anytime you possibly can and for as long as you possibly could. By contrast, a cat — while simply adoring petting — cares deeply about the when and the how much. Don't worry, you won't have to read your cat's mind on this. Approach kitty slowly and put out your hand near his cheek or other favorite spot; proceed unless kitty turns away, pulls in, bites or mimics biting. Don't forget to *stop* petting your cat for the same reasons.

A NOTE ABOUT YOUNGER CHILDREN AND KITTY

It is a very common and extremely unfortunate reality that young children often shower cats with too much of the wrong kind of attention. We've all observed an annoyed cat rushing away to safety from a well-meaning toddler who insists on following kitty *everywhere!* Besides the stress involved in trying to escape, the cat — if caught — usually must endure unwanted petting or holding. Parents, listen up: You are doing your cat and your child a disservice by allowing this pattern to continue! Kitty will react negatively in one way or another (striking out at your child, becoming ornery, hiding, growing fearful or discontent) and your child will not learn early in life the value of respecting animals. Ultimately, you show your cat just how much you love and respect it by teaching your family what to do and what not to do when it comes to cats.

PICKING UP KITTY

Some cats love to be picked up. Others will rarely tolerate it. Most cats fall somewhere in between. One thing is sure: if something pleasant happens to kitty when he or she is picked up, kitty will grow to endure it or even like it! For instance, if you carry kitty to a favorite window ledge or other favorite place, massage his neck or just pet him and talk to him when you pick him up, he'll associate it with positive stuff. Of course if kitty is snuggled up somewhere, be kind and don't disturb him. Also, remember to help your cat become accustomed to being picked up and handled while it is still a kitten — this will make a huge difference later on.

"Ultimately, you show your cat
just how much you love and respect it
by teaching your family what to do
and what not to do when it comes to cats."

Feel free to gently pick up your cat unless he cries (you'll know: it's a painful meow-cry) or moves away. Never force it. And it's good practice to put kitty down long before he cries to be let down, or wriggles out of your hold. He will more likely look forward to it the next time. Young children, especially, need to become mindful of this potential mishandling.

Cats **LOVE** Kitty Massage

THIS COULD BE NEW to you. Many humans are just discovering the joys of massage, and now we are recommending the fine art of kitty massage! Don't be intimidated by this . . . all it really amounts to is "deep petting" in as many places as your cat desires. After just a couple days of offering massage to your cat, she or he will be begging you for it!

Start with the back of the neck. Firmly but gently rub the neck muscles with your thumb and forefinger; you'll want to kind of roll the skin between your fingers. If your cat is like most cats, he or she will melt right into your hand. After a few days of the neck only, slowly continue down the back . . . and onto the head and chest, if kitty seems to be enjoying it. Stop immediately if kitty cries out or acts frightened. Go back to areas you're sure are safe. Always proceed very slowly and let your cat set the boundaries. Kitty massage is a perfect way to say "I love you" to your cat. It's also a fabulous way to make friends with a cat you hardly know.

*"Kittens find much security
and warm fuzzies by kneading."*

Cats LOVE to Knead

THIS IS AN UNUSUAL but endearing method of showing affection. As young, nursing kittens, cats help to stimulate their mothers' milk flow by kneading her underside with a pummeling action of the paws. Kittens find much security and warm fuzzies by kneading.

When given a chance, most cats will daily massage the soft places of his or her most beloved human companion. If this has happened to you, feel honored! There is no doubt that cats love to knead and feel very loved by being allowed to knead, but this exchange of affection is entirely optional. Claws digging into the skin are the major drawback . . . so it's best to let kitty knead you only when you're in thicker clothing or when you've got a blanket or throw for protection.

Cats LOVE Rubs and Kisses

WHEN YOU START GIVING the cat in your life rubs and kisses, your cat may well start giving them to *you*. Simply rub your chin and cheeks against kitty's chin and cheeks. At first, kitty may not grasp what you're trying to do . . . but don't give up. Try getting down on kitty's level and putting your face closer and closer if he's comfortable; but don't smother kitty or over-do it! Since mother cats show affection to their kittens in this way, it is a wonderful and familiar way to bond with your cat.

A FINAL NOTE

ALWAYS STAY MINDFUL OF *the fact that your cat is still a somewhat wild, exotic animal you have chosen to keep as a domestic pet. That cats make this transition as well as they do is a great tribute to feline intelligence and their sincere desire for human companionship. Never forget that every "good" or "right" thing your cat does is because it wants to — not because it thinks it should. Prove to kitty that you respect her unequivocally and she will want to accommodate your requests more often . . . simply in the name of friendship.*

Refer to these pages often, but don't stop here! This book is meant to draw you irresistibly into the heart and mind of the feline, with the hope that your understanding of cats will forever be changed and your interest in them piqued. Read as much as you can about cats. Talk to cat lovers and visit cat shows. Share your kitty adventures with fellow cat owners.

Delve deep into the world of the feline and prepare to become enchanted by these awesome creatures. Surround yourself with one or more kitties and discover why it has been said that a cat has no master . . . just friends.